CW00327649

'Turbinia', the first turbine-powered ship, was built by Charles Parsons in 1894. She demonstrated the practicality of steam turbines and they were fitted to deep-sea ships within a decade of her first trials. She is currently preserved at Exhibition Park, Newcastle upon Tyne (her builder's city).

HISTORIC SHIPS

M. K. Stammers

Shire Publications Ltd

CONTENTS

Set in 9 point Times roman and printed in Great Britain by C. I. Thomas & Sons (Haverfordwest) Ltd, Press Buildings, Merlins Bridge, Haverfordwest, Dyfed.

British Library Cataloguing in Publication Data available.

COVER: *The RRS 'Discovery' and, in the foreground, the figurehead of HMS 'Unicorn', in Victoria Dock, Dundee.*

LEFT: *Little is known about ancient vessels. Most of the detail of this model of a Roman cargo ship was gleaned from carvings in Rome. Underwater archaeology has opened new possibilities for improving our knowledge by excavating shipwrecks. The Blackfriars ship of AD 200, discovered in 1963 and now in the Museum of London, proved there was a native Celtic tradition of boatbuilding as well as the Roman one.*

The techniques and traditions of deep-sea sailing in large square-rigged ships are kept alive by the growing number of sail training ships. The "Tall Ships Races', many of which start or finish in British ports, are a good opportunity to see these training ships under sail and in port. This picture shows the Swedish schooner 'Gladan' with the Danish ship 'Georg Stage' in the background at Liverpool at the end of the 1984 Tall Ships Race.

INTRODUCTION

People have navigated the coastal and inland waters of the British Isles for thousands of years. Recently interest has been increasing in Britain's nautical inheritance. Spectacular archaeological and restoration projects have been accomplished such as the salvage of the *Great Britain* from the Falklands and the raising of the *Mary Rose*. Many ports have their own maritime museums and there is a growing interest in keeping old vessels afloat and working whether they be sail, steam or motor. Ships and boats are some of the largest and most complex of all man-made objects and exist in the corro-

sive environment of the sea, so the costs of ship preservation are very great and some ships such as the famous aircraft carrier *Ark Royal* were too big to be realistic objects for a long-term preservation. Where original vessels have not been preserved, scale models are held by many museums. These can provide a very accurate record in miniature of the features of a ship that has long since gone to the breaker's yard.

This book offers a brief account of how ships have developed and a gazetteer of historic ships and maritime museums.

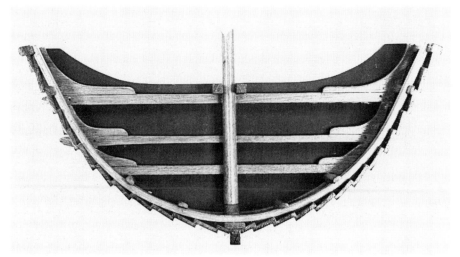

Cross-section of a clinker-built ship of the Scandinavian tradition. The Sutton Hoo and Graveney boats were built in this way, as were the cogs of the middle ages.

EARLY YEARS

The first mariners probably used dugouts (hollowed-out tree trunks). Many of these have been discovered entombed in the mud of rivers and have been preserved in local museums: Warrington in Cheshire has a notable collection. Unfortunately it is impossible to date most of them. The next stage of development was the addition of planks to the sides of the dugout to make it more seaworthy. The three North Ferriby boats are examples of this stage and date from the bronze age, about 1500 BC. The largest is 43 feet (13 metres) long. Two hollowed-out logs form the keel and planks are sewn on with strips of yew. The evidence of traded goods shows that the people of the British Isles were making extensive trading voyages in fully planked boats, probably with sails, before the Roman conquest (AD 55). The Blackfriars ship, a locally designed river sailing barge of about AD 200, now in the Museum of London, gives an idea of what these Celtic ships were like.

The Anglo-Saxons were also great mariners. One of the richest archaeological finds of the twentieth century is the Sutton Hoo ship burial, made in honour of a seventh-century East Anglian chief.

A wealth of information about this large wooden rowing boat was obtained from the 'shadow' of its woodwork left in the sand. A significant advance on the Sutton Hoo boat was the Graveney boat, discovered in 1971 during a marsh drainage scheme in Kent. This vessel dates from about 1000 and could carry a substantial cargo under sail. The Graveney boat owes its design to the Vikings, who from about AD 700 came from Scandinavia first to raid and then to settle in the British Isles. They were great seafarers and their ships were amongst the most outstanding wooden vessels ever built. Two fine examples, the Oseberg and Skuldelev ships, are preserved at Oslo in Norway. Clinker-built, with a single mast and sail, the Viking ships set a pattern that was followed for many centuries.

English ships of the middle ages developed from these Scandinavian origins. One of the dominant kinds of trading vessel of the early medieval period was the *cog*, a considerable improvement on its predecessors. It was a clinker-built ship, decked with a raised superstructure, and had a rudder instead of a steering oar, but still a single mast and sail. A cog found at Bremen in the river Weser in

1961 has been restored and is at the German National Maritime Museum at Bremerhaven. The present-day Humber keel *Comrade* with her single mast, square sails and bluff hull may be a descendent of medieval vessels of this type.

Ship history in this early period is often speculative because contemporary records are scarce, poor and contradictory.

Archaeological discoveries of ships have, however, improved our knowledge a great deal and the best place to study the earliest British ships is the Boat Archaeology Gallery at the National Maritime Museum, Greenwich, where there are reconstructions of the North Ferriby, Sutton Hoo and Graveney boats.

SAILING SHIPS

In the late fourteenth century there occurred a fusion of two different traditions of ship design: the Scandinavian, using square sails for good driving power, and the Mediterranean, with *lateen* (triangular) sails suspended along the centre line (fore and aft) of the ship for working to windward. These two types of sail were combined to form a versatile three-masted rig on a hull built with a heavy internal skeleton and *carvel* (not overlapping) planking. This type of ship is called a *carrack* and in spite of its top-heavy appearance with huge fo'c'sle and after superstructure it was capable of long voyages across the Atlantic, to the Far East and even right round the world. The design was refined over the next three centuries. The surviving vessel nearest in design to a carrack is the Tudor warship *Mary Rose*.

The carrack was superseded by the *galleon*, a more seaworthy craft, and this in turn developed under Dutch influence in the seventeenth century into the classic three-masted sailing ship with three or more square sails on each mast and with multiple fore and aft sail on the bowsprit (which projects in front of the vessel) and between the masts to make windward manoeuvres easier. Tonnage increased from about 100 or 150 in the early seventeenth century to about 400 or 500 by 1800.

Sailing ship design reached its peak with the large fast wooden ships of the mid nineteenth century intended for specific highly profitable trades such as carrying emigrants to Australia and tea from the Far East. A survivor from this era is the *Cutty Sark* of 1869. This vessel incorporated the latest design features,

Wooden sailing ships carried the bulk of British cargoes until as late as the 1870s. Only three survive: the 'Cutty Sark' (at Greenwich) and the 'Carrick' (at Glasgow), both composite ships with iron frames and wood planking, and the 'Jhelum' (shown here) lying as an abandoned store at Stanley in the Falkland Islands. She was a three-masted ship (later a barque) built at Liverpool in 1849. With a cargo capacity of about 500 tons, she was typical of the ocean-going ships of her day.

LEFT: *Cross-section of a carvel-built ship. This was the pattern for seagoing ships by the time of the building of Henry VIII's battleship 'Mary Rose' in 1509. Note the heavy internal frame sandwiched between two skins of smooth planking.*

BELOW: *Wooden sailing ships of almost 100 feet (30 metres) long were still being built for coastal trading, though in declining numbers, until the start of the First World War and the ketch 'Emperor' was launched at Chepstow in 1906 for the Bristol Channel trade. By 1920 her sailing rig had been much reduced and she had been fitted with a motor.*

6

An unusual view of the 'Cutty Sark', the only large merchant sailing ship to be properly preserved in the British Isles, at Birkenhead in 1914. Built in 1869 for the tea trade, she became a noted clipper with fast passages to China and Australia. She was sold in 1895 to Portuguese owners, who kept her trading until 1922. Captain Dowman bought her and restored her original rig. Eventually in 1954 she was moved to a special permanent berth at Greenwich.

including a fine lined composite hull (iron frame with wooden planking), with tall masts to carry as much sail as possible to speed the transport of premium tea from China. Perhaps more typical is the wooden ship *Jhelum* built at Liverpool in 1849 and abandoned in the Falklands in 1871. Though now a mastless wreck, she is the most intact of her kind. She has a stout, deep hull designed for cargo capac-

Unfortunately none of the British-built big iron or steel square-riggers has been preserved in the British Isles, but the 'Wavertree' (built at Southampton in 1885) and four others have been preserved in the United States.

ABOVE: *The schooner 'Kathleen and May' was built at Connah's Quay in 1901 — one of the last wooden sailing vessels to be built. After a long trading career she was restored by the Maritime Trust and is now open to the public at St Mary Overy Dock, London.*

OPPOSITE: *The problems of preserving even medium-sized wooden vessels are immense. They are usually at the end of their working life and often neglected. Water can penetrate the decks and rot the internal frames. The schooner 'Australia' at Mystic Seaport Museum in the United States looks fine from the outside (above), but note how much is rotten when the planking was stripped off below.*

ity rather than speed and is very similar overall to ships of a hundred years earlier.

As well as the deep-sea ships there were fleets of smaller, coastal vessels. Some types, like the Thames barge and the Norfolk wherry, developed in particular areas and had characteristics of hull or rig peculiar to their area. Other types, like the *schooner,* were found all round the coast as well as in certain deep-sea trades. The schooner had mainsails fore and aft on two or three masts, making it easy to sail into and out of estuaries and small havens. Many schooners also carried some square sails on the foremasts. Schooners with auxiliary engines continued to trade until the 1950s and several have been preserved, notably the *Kathleen and May* of 1900, fully restored and owned by the Maritime Trust. Apart from the schooner there were many other types of rig used in coastal trade, ranging from single-masted sloops to square-sailed brigs and brigantines.

Although steamships were working reliably by the 1840s sailing ships remained prevalent until the 1880s. The later sailing ships were built of iron or steel instead of wood and were considerably larger, being designed to work in bulk trades such as grain and coal. They saved on crew by using metal masts and rigging, changing to barque rig (no square sails on the sternmost mast), subdividing the larger sails and equipping with labour-saving devices such as winches. They survived in dwindling numbers until the 1930s, mainly under the Finnish flag. Several British-built or British-owned examples survive, such as the *Wavertree* (1886) in New York, the *Elissa* (1877) in Galveston, Texas, and the *Pommern* (1903) in the Aland Islands in the Baltic Sea.

The schooner 'De Wadden' represents an intermediate stage between the sailing ship and the motor vessel. Built in Holland in 1917, she had a full rig and a diesel engine. Many schooners had diesels fitted retrospectively but the 'De Wadden' was fitted from new. She was sold to the Hall family of Arklow in Ireland after the First World War and carried cargoes across the Irish Sea, including this load of pit props from the river Blackwater to Garston on the Mersey. She is being restored by the Merseyside Maritime Museum.

Paddle tugs were among the first steamers. They continued to be built into the twentieth century. The last were those ordered by the Royal Navy for handling aircraft carriers in the 1950s. Paddles make a ship very manoeuvrable. The 'Old Trafford' was built in 1907 to assist cargo ships in the Manchester Ship Canal. She was sold to Seaham on the north-east coast in 1950 and renamed 'Reliant'. She is now the centrepiece of the Neptune Hall at the National Maritime Museum.

STEAM AND MOTOR SHIPS

The earliest steamers were canal boats powered by paddles, the first being a catamaran with one paddle between the two hulls built in 1788. The *Charlotte Dundas,* a paddle steamer of 1802, plied successfully on the Forth and Clyde Canal and was the first practical application of steam propulsion but was prevented from realising her commercial potential because of fears that her wash would erode the banks of the canal. In 1812 the Clyde steamer *Comet* became the first steam craft to trade on tidal waters and from then onwards there was a growing use of paddle steamers for ferry and coastal services. By 1830, the year of the opening of the first main-line railway, that between Liverpool and Manchester, steamers linked Britain with Europe and Ireland and had also been found to serve well as tugs, towing sailing ships into and out of port. At the end of the decade, the first attempts were being made to cross the Atlantic by steam. Notable steamships included Brunel's paddle steamer *Great Western,* which just failed to become the first to cross the Atlantic under steam westward, and the cross-channel steamer *Sirius* (1838). Although there were many attempts to establish a steamer service across the Atlantic, only Samuel Cunard was successful. He not only had the assistance of a brilliant marine engineer, Robert Napier, but he also gained the contract to carry mail which subsidised the high running costs of his ships. The side-lever paddle engines were run on low-pressure steam generated in primitive boilers and were very wasteful of coal. It was difficult

11

ABOVE: *Recovering the SS 'Great Britain' from the Falklands, where she had been abandoned, was a major feat of salvage. Since 1971 she has been in the dock at Bristol in which she was built and the programme to restore her to her original appearance is continuing. Preserving ships of her size is costly and time-consuming. The scale of her fitting can be appreciated in this deck view, which was taken in the Falklands before the rescue.*

RIGHT: *SS 'Great Britain', restored. Since she arrived at Bristol as a mastless hulk, her restoration has been a long and painstaking project; further work includes fitting out cabin interiors and a full-size set of replica engines.*

RIGHT: *Coal consumption by steamers was improved by higher steam pressures and the triple expansion engine in the early 1880s. Engines of this type with their cylinders above the crankshaft reached massive size with the increase of ships' tonnage. This pair was being built for the White Star liner 'Oceanic', completed by Harland and Wolff in 1899 and the biggest ship since the unfortunate Great Eastern.*

BELOW: *The 'Spartan', a Clyde puffer, was converted from steam to diesel propulsion in 1961 while owned by Glenlight Shipping. She was the first ship to be acquired by the Scottish Maritime Museum at Irvine.*

Tankers have less appeal to the preservationist than a tug or a sailing ship, although their role in twentieth-century shipping is far more significant. The Scottish Maritime Museum has a small coastal tanker, the 'Kyles', and the Ulster Folk and Transport Museum has preserved the little sludge tanker 'Divis' of 1928.

to find room for cargo and passengers as well as space for the large amount of coal needed.

Despite the fuel problem steamer design made rapid progress and Brunel's second ship, the *Great Britain,* was a highly innovative design. She could be called the forerunner of all modern ships. Completed at Bristol in 1843, she was not only the largest ship of her time but she also had an iron instead of a wooden hull, was powered by the more efficent screw propeller at her stern instead of by paddles and had many new safety features including a double bottom and watertight bulkheads to subdivide the hull. After long service first as an Atlantic liner, then as an auxiliary steamer on the Australian run and finally as a sailing ship and storage hulk, she was brought back to her building dock at Bristol for restoration.

Sailing ships were gradually forced out of carrying passengers and high-value goods on the shorter routes, for example across the Atlantic and to the Mediterranean, but remained dominant on long-haul voyages, for example to the Far East, until the 1870s. Brunel built a huge ship, the *Great Eastern*, six times larger than any previous ship, which could carry

all the fuel needed for a voyage to Australia and had space left over for a paying cargo, but she was never a success although she played an important role in laying undersea telegraph cables. Brunel and his vessels helped change ship design from a conservative art into a science.

Improvements in the economy of steam engines and boilers by using higher pressures and compound and later triple expansion engines in ships of the 2000 to 3000 ton range proved to be the way forward. The *Agamemnon* of 1865, designed and built for Alfred Holt, had compound engines and could steam 8000 miles (13,000 km) without coaling. She was the first steamer to compete successfully in the lucrative Far East trade. The opening of the Suez Canal in 1869 and the establishment of a worldwide network of coaling stations enabled the cargo steamer to trade profitably with all continents. There were cargo liners that ran to a regular timetable and tramp steamers that went wherever they could get a cargo.

New kinds of ship were developed to carry new cargoes. Oil was originally carried in barrels or tins in sailing ships. By 1890 there were tankers that carried this increasingly important commodity in bulk. Other vessels were fitted with refrigerating equipment to carry perishable foodstuffs such as meat from South America or Australia. Steel, a far stronger material, displaced wrought iron as the main material for building ships.

In the early twentieth century steam turbines and diesel engines were successfully applied to ships. The pioneer turbine vessel, the steam launch *Turbinia* of 1894, has been preserved at Newcastle upon Tyne. Ships increased in size and the largest of them, the great transatlantic passenger liners such as the Cunard Line's *Mauretania* and the White Star Line's *Titanic,* exceeded the tonnage of the *Great Eastern.*

Oil was found to be a more efficient fuel and easier to handle than coal and many steamers were converted to use it but diesel engines were few until after the 1930s. Early examples were often complicated and not especially reliable. One landmark in their progress was the building of the new 27,000 ton White Star liner *Britannic* with twin diesels instead of turbines in 1930. Diesel engines are the predominant form of propulsion for all merchant ships today and their fuel economy has been greatly improved as a result of the oil crisis of the 1970s.

The Second World War put a huge strain on the British merchant fleet. A vast tonnage of ships was sunk by submarines whilst carrying materials across the Atlantic. Sufficient replacements could only be delivered by the adoption of standard designs and the welding of hulls instead of the traditional fastening method of riveting. Thousands of standard ships were turned out on both sides of the Atlantic and the mass-production methods were adopted elsewhere, especially in the rapidly expanding shipbuilding countries of the Far East, principally Japan.

After the war larger and more specialised ships were developed to cater for increasing trade. Oil tankers (VLCCs, very large crude carriers), grew to enormous and unwieldy sizes of up to half a million tons. The traditional tramp steamer was replaced by bulk carriers transporting coal, grain and similar commodities in consignments of over 100,000 tons. At the same time general cargo liners, which had hitherto carried a wide mixture of goods which demanded great skill and a lot of time to load and discharge, began to change. By the late 1960s on the major routes mixed traffic cargoes were being carried in standard-size steel boxes, or containers. Each new container ship displaced about six of the older type of cargo liner. The steel boxes could be loaded and unloaded very rapidly, usually with the assistance of giant shore cranes. There was also a great increase in wheeled traffic carried at sea and ro/ro (roll on/roll off) ships carry most of the trade between Britain and the European mainland as well as deep-sea business such as bringing motor cars from Japan. The passenger liners had been made redundant by jet aircraft by the late 1960s. Surviving liners such as the *Queen Elizabeth 2* and the *Canberra* now work as cruise ships.

Modern deep-sea ships are probably too big to consider preserving, and indeed many have been designed for a working career of no more than fifteen years, but the smaller ships that serve ports and coastal routes can perhaps be saved. Steam tugs have been rescued and restored in fair numbers and small passenger steamers, which often reflect the decor and facilities of their larger sisters, have also received much attention. A number survive as static club ships, with no attempt to retain either the original appearance or fittings. The most successful project has been the paddle steamer *Waverley*, which has a summer programme of sailings all round the British Isles. Motor ships do not seem to have the same attraction as steam but at least one substantial vessel of an earlier generation has been saved: the Liverpool pilot boat *Edmund Gardner* of 1953.

FOLLOWING PAGE: *Steam turbines were developed by Charles Parsons in the 1890s in his experimental steam launch 'Turbinia', which is preserved at Newcastle upon Tyne. Progress with this new propulsion system was so great that within a decade it was fitted to the largest liners, the Cunard line's express ships 'Mauretania' and 'Lusitania' of 1907. This unusual view of the 'Mauretania' shows her in the special dry dock built at Liverpool for her and her sister ship and emphasises her huge size.*

The most important innovation in twentieth-century naval warfare has been the submarine. Submarines almost brought about the defeat of the Allies in both world wars. Nuclear-powered submarines carrying nuclear missiles have the power to wipe out whole nations. The Royal Navy Submarine Museum at Gosport covers all facets of submarine history and has preserved an A class submarine, HMS 'Alliance' of 1946.

WARSHIPS

Medieval naval warfare was an extension of land battles. Soldiers fought hand to hand on converted merchant ships. The specialised warship developed in the fifteenth century with the introduction of guns. Tactics were transformed because the enemy could be engaged at a distance.

A large section of the hull of Henry VIII's battleship *Mary Rose,* lost in the Solent in 1545, together with much of her twenty-gun main battery, her equipment and her crew's possessions, has been rescued and preserved. She had most of the features of later sailing warships: a heavy battery of muzzle-loading guns firing solid shot through gunports low down along the sides of the hull; extra size (600 tons) and strength; and a full sailing rig. Fighting was often carried on in setpiece actions between fleets of warships. These wooden sailing warships became a major weapon not just for defence but for promoting British interests in trade and empire. They were in constant use in recurring naval wars against rival nations — France, Holland and Spain — in the seventeenth and eighteenth centuries. They were costly to build and used up scarce timber resources, they needed a professional naval service to sail them and they needed permanent dockyards to maintain them. The older buildings of Portsmouth and especially Chatham dockyards are striking evidence of the scale of operation. Battles were fought by lines of battleships, each of which could carry over a hundred guns in three decks. One such ship, HMS *Victory* of 1765, has survived and is a superb example of the high point of wooden warship design, as well as being a memorial to Lord Nelson, who was killed aboard her at the battle of Trafalgar in 1805. The navy also employed smaller warships for scouting, commerce raiding and a whole range of duties outside the competence of the slower, bigger battleships. Two of these frigates, HMS *Foudroyant* (formerly *Trincomalee*) of 1817 and HMS *Unicorn* of 1824, have also survived.

It took longer for steam propulsion to be applied to warships than to merchant ships because paddle wheels were vulnerable to gunfire, but with the successful development of the screw propeller steam engines began to be fitted to the main battle fleet. They were auxiliaries designed to improve the performance of the well tried wooden sailing warship. Explosive shells were a great incentive to change to iron hulls. The first all-metal battleship, HMS *Warrior,* of 9210 tons, was launched on the Thames in 1860 and outclassed all existing warships. Her heavy construction secured her survival after active service and she has undergone restoration to her original appearance.

Sail continued as part of the propulsion system of warships as late as the 1880s in spite of huge improvements in steam engines. Its value was questionable except in keeping up tradition. The Royal Navy enjoyed immense prestige and had a worldwide role but its power was regularly seen to be challenged by the growth of other navies and new developments in weapons. Breach-loading guns in rotating turrets could fling huge high-explosive shells miles rather than yards. The new self-propelled torpedo put great destructive capability into small fast torpedo boats and especially into a new kind of underwater warship, the submarine, which has dominated twentieth-century naval warfare.

At the beginning of the twentieth century naval thinking was still based on the use of larger armoured battleships in fleet actions. In 1906 HMS *Dreadnought,* over 20,000 tons, with 24 knot steam turbines, 12 inch (302 mm) armour plate and twelve 12 inch guns, made all existing battleships obsolete. The battle of Jutland, the only fleet action of the First World War, proved such giant ships were vulnerable and too expensive to commit to massed battles. Submarine warfare against merchant ships bringing supplies across the Atlantic almost brought about defeat for Britain. The use of aircraft for observation and for attack also made the larger ships vulnerable. Subsequent technological advances have extended the range at which ships can be located and attacked. Radar and sonar (for underwater search) were developed during the Second World War and since then guided missiles and jet aircraft have made it possible to engage the enemy beyond the horizon. Battleships have been discarded in favour of smaller faster ships and the capital ship of today is the submarine with steam turbines powered by a nuclear heat source, capable of high underwater speed for long periods and carrying ballistic missiles with nuclear warheads. None of the giant British battleships has survived the scrapyard but the cruiser HMS *Belfast* (1939) gives an excellent idea of the size and complexity of the older kind of big-gun warship.

Brixham trawlers were almost the last big wooden sailing fishing vessels to be built. They made attractive cruising yachts with plentiful accommodation and about half a dozen survive in sailing condition.

FISHING VESSELS

Fish have been caught from boats in the waters around the British Isles for centuries. In the middle ages fishermen sailed from East Anglian ports to line-fish for cod off Iceland. A great variety of boat designs grew up, each one suited to a particular catch or locality. For example, the shrimping boats of Lancashire (Morecambe Bay prawners) are entirely different in form to the shrimpers from Great Yarmouth. Within each type of boat there may also be many variations according to the predilections of the boatbuilder and the owner. The coble, a fishing boat of the north-east coast, comes in many forms depending on whether it is used from open beaches or from sheltered havens. Modern inshore boats are generally built of steel or glass

fibre, but large wooden craft of up to about 70 feet (21.5 metres) are occasionally built and there are still beaches and havens where traditional wooden boats are worked.

The main methods of catching fish were drift-netting, for surface-feeding fish such as herring, and lines for the sea-bed species. In the early nineteenth century deep-water fishing was transformed by the introduction of trawling. A trawl is a bag-shaped net that is towed on or near the bottom, sweeping up every fish in its path. Fishermen at Brixham in Devon were among the first to build the large powerful sailing vessels needed to tow a trawl.

The growth of population in the nineteenth century increased the demand for fish, leading to the rise of large specialist fishing ports (Hull, Grimsby, Fleetwood, Lowestoft and Aberdeen) with fleets of hundreds of vessels. Steam power was applied to fishing vessels in the late nineteenth century, first in the use of converted paddle tugs as trawlers. Steam trawlers had their catching range extended by the introduction of icemaking plant at their home ports. Vessels drift-net fishing for herring converted to steam a decade after the trawlers. The wooden hull was retained until the 1920s and later boats like the Maritime Trust's *Lydia Eva* (1930) were built of steel. Sailing fishing craft continued to work, especially in inshore waters, but sail was gradually supplemented and then replaced by compact diesel or petrol engines. Over-fishing and the extension of territorial waters have brought a decline in fishing in modern times.

Traditional fishing boats have been extensively recorded and some excellent examples preserved. Some still sail as yachts: the Maritime Trust's Brixham trawler *Provident* (1924) is a good example. Smaller inshore boats such as Morecambe prawners or Colchester oyster smacks survive in substantial numbers and are often raced in summer. Powered craft are also being preserved and an important example is the fishing research ship and trawler *Explorer,* which has been acquired by the Aberdeen Maritime Museum.

Whaling is extinct in British waters. In the eighteenth and nineteenth centuries whales supplied oil for lighting and other products that are today derived from mineral oil. The search for whales extended from the Arctic to the Pacific and the Antarctic. Under sail whaling was a very dangerous activity, with skilled harpoon throwers attacking the whales from open rowing boats. Steam whale ships were introduced in the late nineteenth century and the design of the exploration ship *Discovery* (1901), now preserved at Dundee, one of the major whaling ports, was based on this type of ship.

Tugs were among the last types of ship to be built with steam engines. This, with their small size and their attractive appearance, has made them popular for preservation. The 'Kerne' was built for towing barges on the Thames and later moved to the Mersey for similar work. A group of steam enthusiasts bought her in 1970 and has kept her steaming ever since, although not without a great deal of hard work.

PLEASURE BOATS AND HARBOUR SERVICE VESSELS

Boating for pleasure is a relatively recent pastime. The first English yacht was the *Mary* of 1660 given to Charles II by the Dutch at the time of his restoration to the English throne. Later in his reign he enjoyed racing yachts, and yachting remained an aristocratic pursuit until the growth of yacht clubs in the mid nineteenth century. Standardised rules, handicapping and 'one-design' boats which placed a premium on the skills of the skipper and his crew all became an accepted part of racing. Many vintage yachts have survived and are kept sailing by their dedicated owners. Old 'one-design' classes like the 'brown boats' of the Norfolk Broads or the 'sea birds' of North Wales are still enthusiastically raced. Yacht design has undergone radical change. The days of huge craft with paid crews have gone. Modern yachts have fibreglass hulls and simplified rigging with Bermudan mainsails and a range of other sails for different weather conditions. Dinghy racing in small open boats with centreboards instead of fixed keels was introduced about 1900 and opened the sport to a still wider range of people. Many classes of boat compete and the origins of some, like the International 14, can be traced back to the early days. Not all yachtsmen want to compete in races. Cruising also became popular and since the Second World War yachts have extended their range to encompass the world. Pioneer yachts like Sir Francis Chichester's *Gipsy Moth IV* and Sir Alex Rose's *Lively Lady* have been preserved.

Steam power popularised the pleasures of a sea trip. Excursion steamers became an essential ingredient of the British seaside resort. In their heyday it was possible to cruise right round the British Isles. The very rich owned luxurious steam yachts in which they could cruise where they pleased. In the 1860s improvements in steam engines made small steamboats for lakes and rivers possible and some, like those preserved at the Windermere Steamboat Museum, are as elegant as their larger seagoing counterparts. Some steamboats were used for racing or speed trials but power-boat racing did not achieve its present popularity until the introduction of internal combustion engines. A number of the spectacular record-breaking speedboats have been preserved. There is a growing movement to preserve small steamboats and to build new ones, and the old seaside steamer trip can still be enjoyed on the last seagoing paddle steamer, the *Waverley*, which makes many calls along the west and south coasts in the summer.

Harbour service vessels include such craft as tugs, dredgers, floating cranes, pilot vessels, survey ships, sludge disposal ships, ferries and buoy tenders. As they all operated in relatively sheltered waters and often for limited periods they tended to outlast their commercial and deep-sea sisters and so many steamers survived to the 1970s when the ship preservation movement was gathering momentum. Thus a substantial number of tugs has been preserved (that is also a reflection of their comparatively small size), as well as at least two steam dredgers, two steam sludge disposal ships, with a third still working as a motor ship, and half a dozen lightships. Although they lack the glamour of bigger ships they incorporate many of their features on a smaller, more practicable scale.

'Elswick No. 2' under restoration. This Tyne barge is probably the largest surviving clinker-built vessel in the British Isles. She has something of the character of the clinker-built ships of the middle ages except that she never sailed but was always towed. She is part of the Maritime Trust's collection and is kept on the Tyne in the charge of the Tyne and Wear Museums Service.

The 'Esperance' was built for the great Victorian industrialist Sir James Ramsden to travel from his Windermere home down the lake to the railway station to catch his own train to the steel and shipbuilding town of Barrow-in-Furness, where he worked. The 'Esperance' is part of the Windermere Steamboat Museum collection.

ORGANISATIONS

Humber Keel and Sloop Preservation Society, c/o Glenlea, Main Road, New Ellerby, North Humberside. Preserves and sails the sloop *Amy Howson* (1914) and the Humber keel *Comrade;* both have summer programmes and are available for charter.

Mariners International, c/o National Maritime Museum, Romney Road, Greenwich, London SE10 9NF. An association for people interested in sailing historic ships, especially square-riggers.

The Maritime Trust, 16 Ebury Street, London SW1W 0LH. Telephone: 01-730 0096. The national organisation for ship preservation owns the following vessels: *Barnabas* (Cornish fishing lugger, 1881), sailing at Falmouth; *Blossom* (north-eastern fishing mule, 1871), on loan to the Museum of Science and Engineering, Newcastle upon Tyne; *Cambria* (Thames sailing barge, 1906); *Cutty Sark* (clipper, 1869), at Greenwich; *Discovery* (royal research ship, 1901), at Dundee; *Ellen* (crabber, about 1882), under restoration at Falmouth; *Elswick No. 2* (Tyne wherry, 1930s), on loan to the Museum of Science and Engineering, Newcastle upon Tyne; *Gannet* (auxiliary steam sloop, 1878), under restoration at Chatham; *Gipsy Moth IV* (yacht, 1966), at Greenwich; *Hope* (National 14 dinghy number 1); *HSL (S) 376* (Admiralty harbour service launch, 1944), at the Maritime Workshop, Gosport; *Kathleen and May* (topsail schooner, 1901), in St Mary Overy Dock near London Bridge; *Kindly Light* (pilot cutter, 1904), at the Welsh Industrial and Maritime Museum, Cardiff; *Lively Lady* (yacht, 1948), at Portsmouth; *Lydia Eva* (steam drifter, 1930); *Peggy* (Sunderland foyman's coble, 1890), on loan to the Museum of Science and Engineering, Newcastle upon Tyne; *Portwey* (tug, 1927); *Provident* (trawler, 1924), at the Island Cruising Club, Salcombe, Devon; *Robin* (steam coaster, 1890); *Soft Wings* (oyster dredger, 1910), sailing at Falmouth; *Steam Cutter number 463* (tender to royal yacht, 1899), at the Maritime Workshop, Gosport. Some vessels from the collection may be berthed for exhibition at the West India Dock, London.

The Maritime Workshop, Gosport, Hampshire. A young people's training centre undertaking major restoration projects on steamboats.

Norfolk Wherry Trust: Honorary Secretary, 63 Whitehall Road, Norwich, Norfolk NR2 3EN. Owns the wherry *Albion.*

Old Gaffers Association: Honorary Secretary, M. Burn, Grove Farm House, Little Bealings, Woodbridge, Suffolk IP13 6LT. For owners of gaff-rigged sailing craft and other enthusiasts; organises races and rallies.

Ships Preservation Ltd, The Custom House, Victoria Terrace, Hartlepool, Cleveland. Telephone: Hartlepool (0429) 33051.

Steam Boat Association: Honorary Secretary, 19 Millbank, Kintbury, Berkshire. For steamboat owners and enthusiasts; organises rallies and publishes *The Funnel and Steamboat Index.*

GAZETTEER OF HISTORIC SHIPS AND MARITIME MUSEUMS

This list includes vessels that are preserved and museums with maritime collections. It is as comprehensive as possible but some museums and preservation schemes are still developing and not yet fully open to visitors. Intending visitors should find out the times of opening before making a special journey. Ships marked with an asterisk are not open to the public.

AVON

Bristol Industrial Museum, Prince's Wharf, Prince Street, Bristol BS1 4RN. Telephone: Bristol (0272) 299771. The steam tug *May* (1861), the oldest working tug.

National Lifeboat Museum, Prince's Wharf, Wapping Road, Bristol BS1 4RN. Telephone: Bristol (0272) 213389.

SS Great Britain, Great Western Dock, Gas Ferry Road, Bristol BS1 6TY. Telephone: Bristol (0272) 20680. Brunel's screw-propelled iron ship of 1843 rescued from the Falklands in 1971 and undergoing restoration in the dock in which she was built.

William McCann. A Hull sailing trawler brought back from the Faroe Islands for restoration and in sailing condition; mainly based on Bristol.

CAMBRIDGESHIRE

Cambridge Museum of Technology, Riverside, Newmarket Road, Cambridge. Telephone: Cambridge (0223) 68650. *Black Prince,* a Fenland barge, excavated 1974.

Imperial War Museum, Duxford Airfield, Duxford, Cambridge CB2 4QR. Telephone: Cambridge (0223) 833963. Two First World War motorboats.

CHESHIRE

The Boat Museum, Dockyard Road, Ellesmere Port L65 4EF. Telephone 051-355 5017. The largest collection of inland craft in Europe, ranging from narrowboats to the Manchester Ship Canal steamer *Daniel Adamson* (1903), the puffer *Basuto* (1902) and the privately owned steam dredger *Mannin 2,* in the restored dock terminus of the Shropshire Union Canal. The steam tug *Kerne** (1913), owned by the North Western Steam Ship Company, is based here and at the Merseyside Maritime Museum, Liverpool.

CLEVELAND

Captain Cook Birthplace Museum, Stewarts Park, Middlesbrough. Telephone: Middlesbrough (0642) 311211.

Hartlepool Maritime Museum, Northgate, Hartlepool. Telephone: Hartlepool (0429) 272814.

The Zetland Museum, King Street, Redcar. Telephone: Redcar (0642) 71921. The pioneer lifeboat *Zetland* (1800).

CORNWALL

Bude Historical and Folk Exhibition, The Old Forge, Lower Wharf, Bude. Telephone: Bude (0288) 3576. Includes a wheeled tub boat from the Bude Canal.

Falmouth Maritime Museum, 2 Bell's Court, Falmouth. Telephone: Falmouth (0326) 318107 or 250507. The museum owns the tug *St Denys* (1929), moored at Custom House Quay, Falmouth. The Maritime Trust fishing vessels *Barnabas** (mackerel driver, 1881), *Ellen** (crabber, about 1882) and *Soft Wings* (oyster dredger, 1910) are also based at Falmouth.

National Maritime Museum Outstation, Cotehele Quay, St Dominick, Saltash PL12 6TA. Telephone: Liskeard (0579) 50830. The river Tamar barge *Shamrock* (1899), fully restored to sailing condition, is moored here.

Valhalla Figurehead Collection, Abbey Gardens, Tresco, Isles of Scilly. Telephone: Scillonia (0720) 22849. Ships' figureheads and carvings from local shipwrecks.

CUMBRIA

Furness Museum, Ramsden Square, Barrow-in-Furness, Cumbria LA14 1LL. Telephone: Barrow-in-Furness (0229) 20650.

Gondola (steam launch, 1859), Coniston. Telephone: Coniston (0966) 58075. Makes regular trips on the lake.

Maryport Maritime Museum, 1 Senhouse Street, Shipping Brow, Maryport, Cumbria CA15 6AB. Telephone: Maryport (090 081) 3738. Note also the restored docks with the steam yacht *Scharnhorn,* a steam tug, a puffer and the ketch *Emily Barratt* (1914).

Whitehaven Museum and Art Gallery, Market Place, Whitehaven, Cumbria CA28 7JG. Telephone: Whitehaven (0946) 3111 extension 307. The steam dredger *Clearway** (1927) is in Whitehaven harbour.

Windermere Steamboat Museum, Rayrigg Road, Windermere, Cumbria LA23 1BN. Telephone: Windermere (096 62) 5565. Probably the finest collection of steam launches in the world, most of which, including *Dolly* (1850), are in working order.

The fine steam tug 'St Canute' is one of the major exhibits of the Exeter Maritime Museum. She was built in Denmark in 1931 and worked in the Cornish port of Fowey from 1958 to 1969, when she was brought to Exeter for preservation.

DEVON

Arlington Court, Arlington, near Barnstaple EX31 4LP. Telephone: Shirwell (027 182) 296. A stately home with a noted collection of French prisoner-of-war models.

British Fisheries Museum, Old Market House, The Quay, Brixham. Telephone: Brixham (080 45) 2861.

Brixham Museum, Bolton Cross, Brixham TQ5 8LZ. Telephone: Paignton (0803) 557129. Incorporates HM Coastguard National Museum.

Exeter Maritime Museum, The Quay, Exeter EX2 4AN. Telephone: Exeter (0392) 58075. A worldwide collection of craft including sailing craft from the Pacific, China and the Middle East, a notable collection of Portuguese boats and some unusual British ones such as the swan-shaped *Cygnet,* the Brunel drag boat *Bertha* (1844), the steam tug *St Canute* (1931) and *Cariad* (1904), a Bristol Channel pilot cutter.

Hartland Quay Museum, near Bideford, Devon EX39 6A. Telephone: Bideford (023 74) 693.

Island Cruising Club, Island Street, Salcombe, Devon. Telephone: Salcombe (054 884) 3481. The Brixham trawler *Provident* (1924) and the schooner yacht *Hoshi* (1909).

Morwellham Quay Open Air Museum, Morwellham, Tavistock PL19 8JL. Telephone: Tavistock (0822) 832766.

North Devon Maritime Museum, Odun House, Odun Road, Appledore. Telephone: Bideford (023 72) 4852.

DORSET

Poole Maritime Museum, Paradise Street, The Quay, Poole BH15 1HJ. Telephone: Poole (0202) 675151. In a fourteenth-century warehouse, boats include X class and International 14 dinghies.

EAST SUSSEX

Fisherman's Museum, Rock-a-Nore, Hastings. Telephone: Hastings (0424) 424787. The Hastings lugger *Enterprise* (1909).

HMS Cavalier (1945), Brighton Marina, Brighton. This sole surviving Second World War destroyer will be moving to Tyneside.

Royal National Lifeboat Institution Museum, Grand Parade, Eastbourne. Telephone: Eastbourne (0323) 30717.

ESSEX

Maldon. Centre for Thames sailing barges with repair yard, restored east coast fishing smacks and the steam tug *Brent** (1945).

GREATER LONDON

Cutty Sark Clipper Ship, King William Walk, Greenwich, London SE10. Telephone: 01-858 3445. The famous clipper ship (1869) in her own dry dock.

Gipsy Moth IV, King William Walk, Greenwich, London SE10. Telephone enquiries to Maritime Trust: 01-730 0096. The yacht in which Sir Francis Chichester sailed round the world, now in the care of the Maritime Trust.

HMS Belfast, Symons Wharf, Vine Lane, London SE1 2JH. Telephone: 01-407 6434.

Kathleen and May, St Mary Overy Dock, Cathedral Street, London SE1 9DE. Telephone: 01-403 3965. A topsail schooner (1901), part of the Maritime Trust collection.

National Maritime Museum, Romney Road, Greenwich, London SE10 9NF. Telephone: 01-858 4422. One of the finest maritime museums in the world, with superb collections. Neptune Hall contains many historic boats, the steam paddle tug *Reliant* and the reconstructions of the early North Ferriby, Sutton Hoo and Graveney boats.

St Katharine's Dock, London E1 9LB. The steam tug *Challenge,* the Nore lightship, the river steamer *Resolute* and Thames barges.

Science Museum, Exhibition Road, South Kensington, London SW7 2DD. Telephone: 01-589 3456. Excellent model and marine engineering collections.

The 'Warrior' being escorted into Portsmouth following her restoration at Hartlepool which lasted from 1979 until 1987. The first iron-hulled warship 'Warrior', built as a frigate, exceeded contemporary battleships in length and displacement.

West India Dock, Poplar, London E14. A substantial part of the Maritime Trust's collection may be berthed for exhibition here, along with the four vessels of the London Docklands Museum, the fire tender *Massey Show* and the steam cable ship *John McKay** (1922).

HAMPSHIRE

Buckler's Hard Maritime Museum and Village Display, Buckler's Hard, Beaulieu, Hampshire. Telephone: Beaulieu (059 063) 203. An eighteenth-century shipbuilding hamlet close to supplies of New Forest oak for warship building. Imaginative reconstructions of interiors of key buildings such as the master shipwright's house and the inn.

HMS Foudroyant* (frigate, 1818). This training ship is to be restored at Hartlepool before returning to Portsmouth harbour.

HMS Warrior, HM Naval Base, Portsmouth. The first of the metal warships (1861).

Lively Lady*, Portsmouth. Telephone Portsmouth City Museums: Portsmouth (0705) 827261. Sir Alec Rose's round-the-world yacht.

Mary Rose Ship Hall and Exhibition, HM Naval Base, Portsmouth. Telephone: Portsmouth (0705) 750521. Substantial remains of Henry VIII's sailing battleship *Mary Rose* (1510).

Royal Marines Museum, Royal Marines Barracks, Eastney, Southsea PO4 9PX. Telephone: Portsmouth (0705) 822351.

Royal Naval Museum and HMS Victory, HM Naval Base, Portsmouth PO1 3LR. Telephone: Portsmouth (0705) 733060. Nelson's flagship at Trafalgar, a superbly preserved first-rate wooden warship (1765). Museum housed in nearby eighteenth-century dockyard warehouses with many Nelson relics.

Royal Navy Submarine Museum, HMS Dolphin, Gosport PO12 2AB. Telephone: Gosport (0705) 529217. The submarine HMS *Alliance* (1945) and the recently raised *Holland I,* (1901), the pioneer submarine of the Royal Navy.

Wool House Maritime Museum, Bugle Street, Southampton. Telephone: Southampton (0703) 23941. Medieval warehouse, some good liner models. Plans in hand for larger waterfront premises to include steam sludge carrier *Shieldhall* (1955) and passenger tender *Calshot* (1930).

HUMBERSIDE

Amy Howson (sloop, 1914). Owned by the Humber Keel and Sloop Preservation Society.

Lincoln Castle*, This paddle steamer (1940), a former Humber ferry, is to be exhibited at Grimsby.

Spurn Lightship, Hull Marina, Hull.

Town Docks Museum, Queen Victoria Square, Hull HU1 3DX. Telephone: Hull (0482) 222737. Former dock office, excellent displays on whaling, local fishing and trade.

The 'Mary Rose' on display in dry dock at Portsmouth Naval Base. It is surrounded by a water sprinkler system to keep the timbers moist and prevent damage from contraction.

ISLE OF WIGHT
Cowes Maritime Museum, Beckford Road, Cowes PO31 7SG. Telephone: Cowes (0983) 293341.
Bembridge Maritime Museum, Bembridge. Telephone: Bembridge (0983) 872223.

KENT
Chatham Historic Dockyard Trust, The Old Pay Office, Church Lane, Chatham Historic Dockyard, Chatham ME4 4TQ. Telephone: Medway (0634) 812551. Splendid collection of eighteenth- and early nineteenth-century dockyard buildings including the covered shipbuilding berths and the ropery and flagloft, which are still in operation. The Maritime Trust's *Gannet* (sail and steam sloop, 1878) is undergoing restoration in Number 3 dry dock.
Dolphin Sailing Barge Museum, Crown Quay Lane, Sittingbourne. Telephone: Maidstone (0622) 62531. Restored barge yard with several Thames sailing barges.
East Kent Maritime Trust, Clock House, Pier Head, Royal Harbour, Ramsgate. Steam tug *Cervia* (1946) and Dunkirk veteran *Sundowner.*
Kingswear Castle, Chatham Historic Dockyard, Chatham. Paddle steamer owned by Paddle Steamer Navigation Ltd, 10 Crescent Rise, Crescent Road, London N3 1HS.
Medway Maritime Museum, Chatham Dockyard, Chatham. Steam paddle tug *John H Amos* (1931) and the tug *Tid 64.*

LANCASHIRE
Fleetwood Museum, Dock Street, Fleetwood. Telephone: Preston (0772) 264062.
Lancaster Maritime Museum, Old Custom House, St George's Quay, Lancaster. Telephone: Lancaster (0524) 64637. An eighteenth-century customs house flanked by eighteenth-century stone warehouses. The collection includes a local whammel boat and prawner.

MERSEYSIDE
Botanic Gardens Museum, Churchtown, Southport PR9 7NB. Telephone: Southport (0704) 27547. Large dugout; galleries on shrimping and local lifeboats.
Merseyside Maritime Museum, Pier Head, Liverpool L3 1DN. Telephone: 051-709 1551. Restored Victorian docks and warehouse, the pilot boat *Edmund Gardner* (1953), the schooner *De Wadden** (1917), the Weaver packet *Wincham** (1946) and the Mersey flat *Oakdale** (1953). Boatbuilding workshop and wooden boats display.

NORFOLK
Albion (Norfolk wherry). Owned by the Norfolk Wherry Trust and based mainly at Womack Water, Wroxham.
Bridewell Museum of Local Industries, Bridewell Alley, Norwich NR2 1AQ. Telephone: Norwich (0603) 611277 extension 299. Good display on Broads boatbuilders and wherries.
The Cromer Museum, East Cottages, Tucker Street, Cromer NR27 9HB. Telephone: Cromer (0263) 513543.
Hales Hall*, near Norwich. A Norfolk keel, the forerunner of the wherry, has been raised and is under conservation.
Lightship*, Riverside Road, Norwich. Owned by Sea Scouts.
Maritime Museum for East Anglia, Marine Parade, Great Yarmouth NR30 2EW. Telephone: Great Yarmouth (0493) 842267. Good collection of models, shipwrights' tools, etc. Boats include the early Broads yacht *Maria* and a Yarmouth beach boat.
Motor Torpedo Boat MTB 102*, Brundall, near Norwich. Restored by local Sea Scouts.

NORTHAMPTONSHIRE
The Waterways Museum, Stoke Bruerne, near Towcester NN12 7SE. Telephone: Northampton (0604) 862229. Canal warehouse, unique boat-weighing machine with narrowboat.

NORTHUMBERLAND
Grace Darling Museum, 1 Radcliffe Road, Bamburgh NE69 7AE. Telephone: Bamburgh (066 84) 310. Preserves the coble used by the heroine and her father to reach the wreck of the *Forfarshire* in 1838.

NORTH YORKSHIRE
Whitby Museum, Pannett Park, Whitby YO21 1RE. Telephone: Whitby (0947) 602908.

SHROPSHIRE
Blists Hill Open Air Museum (Ironbridge Gorge Museum Trust), Coalport Road, Madeley, Telford. Telephone: Telford (0952) 586063. The last Severn trow *Spry* (1894), and an early iron canal tub boat.
Severn Warehouse Visitor Centre (Ironbridge Gorge Museum Trust), The Wharfage, Ironbridge, Telford. Telephone: Ironbridge (095 245) 3522. Display of Severn coracles and coracle making.

SOMERSET
Admiral Blake Museum, Blake Street, Bridgwater. Telephone: Bridgwater (0278) 456127.

SUFFOLK
Constable (river Stour barge, 1820), Quay Street, Sudbury.
Lowestoft and East Suffolk Maritime Museum, Fisherman's Cottage, Sparrows Nest Park, Lowestoft. Telephone: Lowestoft (0502) 61963. Small but good models. Plans for larger premises to include full-size local yacht and fishing vessel.
Southwold Museum, Bartholomews Green, Southwold.

TYNE AND WEAR
Museum of Science and Engineering, Blandford House, West Blandford Street, Newcastle upon Tyne NE1 4JA. Telephone: Newcastle upon Tyne (0632) 326789. Local shipbuilding a speciality with a superb model of the *River Tyne*. Also *Peggy**, *Blossom** and *Elswick No. 2** on loan from Maritime Trust.
Sunderland Museum and Art Gallery, Borough Road, Sunderland SR1 1PP. Telephone: Sunderland (0783) 41235. Good display of models of locally built ships.
Turbinia Hall, Exhibition Park, Newcastle upon Tyne. The pioneer turbine vessel, *Turbinia* (1894). Open only by written appointment with Tyne and Wear Museums Service, Blandford House, West Blandford Street, Newcastle upon Tyne NE1 4JA.

WEST MIDLANDS
Black Country Museum, Tipton Road, Dudley DY1 4SQ. Telephone: 021-557 9643. Working boatyard and narrowboats.

WEST SUSSEX
Marlipins Museum, High Street, Shoreham-by-Sea. Telephone: Shoreham-by-Sea (079 17) 62994.

CHANNEL ISLANDS
Fort Grey, Rocquaine Bay, St Peter's, Guernsey. Telephone: Guernsey (0481) 65036. Maritime museum, shipwrecks.

ISLE OF MAN
Nautical Museum, Bridge Street, Castletown. Telephone: Castletown (0624) 5522. Schooner yacht *Peggy* (1791) in her own dock under the house of her owners the Quayle family, on the edge of the harbour.

NORTHERN IRELAND
Belfast Docks, Belfast. A large collection of local craft including the schooner *Result* (1890), the fishing vessel *Mary Joseph* (1878) from Kilkeel, and the steam sludge vessel *Divis**. At Milewater Basin in the docks is HMS *Caroline** (1914), a First World War cruiser used as a Royal Naval Reserve base.
Ulster Folk and Transport Museum, Cultra Manor, Holywood, County Down BT18 0EU. Telephone: Holywood (023 17) 5411.

SCOTLAND
Aberdeen Maritime Museum, Provost Ross's House, Shiprow, Aberdeen. Telephone: Aberdeen (0224) 585788. Displays including fishing, whaling, shipbuilding, shipwrecks and the North Sea gas and oil industry. An extension is planned and the museum has bought for restoration the last surviving Aberdeen steam trawler, the *Explorer** (1955).
Auld Reekie (VIC27, 1943). A working Clyde puffer based mainly at Oban, Argyll.
Buckie Maritime Museum, Town House West, Cluny Place, Buckie, Banffshire AB5 1HB. Telephone: Forres (0309) 73701.
Carrick*, Glasgow. Royal Naval Volunteer Reserve club ship, formerly the composite sailing ship *City of Adelaide* (1864).
Glasgow Museum of Transport, Kelvin Hall, Glasgow. Telephone enquiries: 041-423 8000. To reopen in 1988. The museum of a major shipbuilding river with a splendid collection of builders' models including the Cunard *Queen* liners.
HMS Unicorn, Victoria Dock, Dundee. 46-gun sailing frigate of 1824; it never saw active service but is well preserved as a Royal Naval Reserve depot ship.
Maid of the Loch*, Balloch Pier, Balloch, Dunbartonshire. A paddle steamer (1953) in use as a landing stage on Loch Lomond.
McLean Museum and Art Gallery, 9 Union Street, West End, Greenock, Renfrewshire PA16 8JH. Telephone: Greenock (0475) 23741.
Nairn Fishertown Museum, Laing Hall, Union Street, Nairn.
Royal Museum of Scotland, Chambers Street, Edinburgh EH1 1JF. Telephone: 031-225 7534. Notable collection of models including an incomparable Dutch East Indiaman of 1719.
RRS Discovery (Dundee Heritage Trust), Victoria Harbour, Dundee. Telephone: Dundee (0382) 25282. An ambitious waterfront project including the Antarctic exploration ship *Discovery,* built here in 1901.
Scottish Fisheries Museum, St Ayles, Harbourhead, Anstruther, Fife KY10 3AB. Telephone: Anstruther (0333) 310628. Displays of small fishing boats and gear in the museum's courtyard and wide-ranging displays on fish and fishing within. In the harbour the fifie *Reaper* of 1901, a 70 foot (21 metre) lug-rigged vessel for drift-netting in full sailing condition and the zulu *Research** await restoration.
Scottish Maritime Museum, Laird Forge, Gottries Road, Irvine, Ayrshire KA12 8QE. Telephone: Irvine (0294) 78283. Growing fleet of ships in harbour including the local tug *Garnock* (1956), the puffer *Spartan* (1942), the tanker *Kyles* (1872), the yachts *Vagrant* (1884) and *Brunette* (1896) and Lord Bute's yacht of 1818, *Lady Guilford*.
Shetland Museum, Lower Hillhead, Lerwick, Shetland ZE1 0EL. Telephone: Lerwick (0595) 5057.
Sir Walter Scott (paddle steamer), Lock Katrine. Enquiries: Strathclyde Water Department, 419 Balmore Road, Glasgow.
Stromness Museum, 52 Alfred Street, Stromness, Orkney KW16 3DF. Telephone: Stromness (0856) 850025.
Waverley (paddle steamer), Waverley Terminal, Stobcross Quay, Glasgow. Telephone: 041-423 8000. The last seagoing paddle steamer, the *Waverley* makes extensive coastal tours of the British Isles in the summer season.

WALES
Gwynedd Maritime Museum, Greaves Wharf, Porthmadog, Gwynedd. The coasting

ketch *Garlandstone* (1909) (likely to move) and a local lifeboat.

Nelson Collection and Local History Centre, Priory Street, Monmouth, Gwent. Telephone: Monmouth (0600) 3519.

Seiont II Maritime Museum, Victoria Dock, Caernarfon, Gwynedd. Telephone: Bangor (0248) 600835. *Seiont II,* 1938 steam dredger in working condition, and local ferry *Nantlys* (1920).

Swansea Maritime and Industrial Museum, Museum Square, Maritime Quarter, Swansea, SA1 1UN. Telephone: Swansea (0792) 50351. Coast Line's warehouse, the steam tug *Canning* (1954), the former sailing smack *Katie Ann* (1921), the Helwick lightship (1927) and a Bristol Channel pilot cutter.

Welsh Industrial and Maritime Museum, Bute Street, Cardiff. Telephone: Cardiff (0222) 481919. Marine exhibits include the steam tug *Sea Alarm* (1941) and the Bristol Channel pilot cutter *Kindly Light* (1904).

OTHER PRESERVED VESSELS

Comrade (Humber keel). Owned by the Humber Keel and Sloop Preservation Society (see Organisations).

Irene* (coasting ketch in sailing condition, 1907). Owner: Dr L. Morrish, Bishops Lodge, Oakley Green, Windsor, Berkshire.

Olive* (wherry yacht). In private ownership in Norfolk.

VIC 32 (Clyde puffer, 1943). Now a holiday cruise ship in steam along the western coast of the Scottish Highlands. Enquiries: c/o The Change House, Crinan Ferry, Lochgilphead, Argyll PA31 8QH. Telephone: Lochgilphead (054 65) 232.

Windsor Belle (restored Thames excursion steamer). Enquiries: c/o 17 Boswell Road, Henley-on-Thames, Oxfordshire.

FURTHER READING

BOOKS

Burton, Anthony. *The Past Afloat.* André Deutsch/BBC, 1982.
Coad, J. G. *Historic Architecture of the Royal Navy.* Gollancz, 1983.
Corlett, E. W. *The Iron Ship.* Moonraker Press, 1976.
Greenhill, Basil. *The Merchant Schooners.* National Maritime Museum (HMSO), reprinted 1978.
Kemp, P. (editor). *The Oxford Companion to Ships and the Sea.* Oxford University Press, 1976.
McKee, Eric. *Working Boats of Britain.* Conway Maritime Press, 1983.
Stammers, M. K. *Steamboats.* Shire Publications, 1986.
Various authors. *The Ship* (ten volumes). National Maritime Museum (HMSO), 1981.

PERIODICALS

Mariner's Mirror (quarterly): Society for Nautical Research, c/o National Maritime Museum.
Maritime Wales (annual): Gwynedd Archives Service, Caernarfon, Gwynedd.
Sea Breezes (monthly): 202 Cotton Exchange Buildings, Old Hall Street, Liverpool.
Ships Monthly: Kottingham House, Dale Street, Burton upon Trent, Staffordshire.

ACKNOWLEDGEMENTS
The author acknowledges with thanks the help given by his wife, by his colleagues at National Museums and Galleries on Merseyside and by all his colleagues in other maritime museums and ship preservation organisations. Illustrations are acknowledged to: Paul Boot, page 21; Bristol Museum, page 6 (lower); Cadbury Lamb, cover and pages 12 (lower), 23, 25; the Maritime Trust, page 9; the *Mary Rose* Trust, page 28; Merseyside Maritime Museum, pages 2, 3, 4, 5, 6 (upper), 7 (both), 11, 12 (upper), 13 (upper), 16, 19; Mystic Seaport, page 8 (both); Royal Navy Submarine Museum, page 17; Scottish Maritime Museum, page 13 (lower); D. Smith, page 10; Tyne and Wear Museums Service, pages 1, 22; Ulster Folk and Transport Museum, page 14; the *Warrior* Preservation Trust, page 27.